Himeji Castle

Japan's Samurai Past

By Jacqueline A. Ball

Consultant: Stephen F. Brown, Director
Institute of Medieval Philosophy and Theology, Boston College

BEARPORT
PUBLISHING COMPANY, INC.

New York, New York

Credits

Cover: Travel Ink / Alamy; 1: Travel Ink / Alamy; 4: Courtesy Tottori Prefecture Museum, Japan; 4-5: Craig Lovell / Corbis; 8: Werner Froman / Corbis; 9: Carmen Redonda / Corbis; 10: Richard Seaman; 11: Richard Seaman; 12: Carmen Redonda / Corbis; 13: Richard Seaman; 14: Werner Forman / Art Resource, NY; 15: SuperStock; 16: Michael S. Yamashita / Corbis; 17: Richard Seaman; 18: Art Resource Inc.; 19: Photofest; 20-21: Courtesy Hyogo Prefecture History Museum, Hidekichi Takahashi Collection, Japan; 22-23: Richard Seaman; 24: Asian Art & Archaeology Inc. / Corbis; 25: Alamy; 26-27: Rodica Prato; 28: Courtesy Hyogo Prefecture History Museum, Japan; 29: Travel Ink / Alamy

Design and production by Dawn Beard Creative, Triesta Hall of Blu-Design, and Octavo Design and Production, Inc.

Library of Congress Cataloging-in-Publication Data

Ball, Jacqueline A.
  Himeji Castle: Japan's samurai past / by Jacqueline A. Ball; consultant, Stephen Brown.
    p. cm. — (Castles, palaces, and tombs)
  Includes bibliographical references and index.
  ISBN 1-59716-001-6 (lib. bdg.) — ISBN 1-59716-024-5 (pbk.)
  1. Himejijo (Himeji-shi, Japan)—History. 2. Castles—Japan—Himeji-shi. 3. Himeji-shi (Japan)—History. 4. Samurai—History. 5. Japan—History—1185-1600. I. Brown, Stephen. II. Title. III. Series.

  DS897.H462B35 2005
  952'.02—dc22

                              2004020987

For more information, write to Bearport Publishing Company, Inc., 101 Fifth Avenue, Suite 6R, New York, New York 10003. Printed in the United States of America.

                      1 2 3 4 5 6 7 8 9 10

Table of Contents

A Warlord's Castle 4

A Reward for Ikeda 6

White Crane Castle 8

Beautiful and Strong 10

Grounds for Defense 12

Always Ready to Fight 14

Secrets Inside 16

Shadow Warriors 18

An Amazing Maze 20

A Palace for a Princess 22

Okiku's Well 24

Visiting Himeji Castle Today 26

Just the Facts 28

Timeline 29

Glossary 30

Bibliography 31

Read More 31

Learn More Online 31

Index 32

About the Author 32

A Warlord's Castle

The Japanese **warlord** Ikeda (ee-kay-duh) stood at the top of a tall tower. From here, attackers could be spotted when they were still far away. The warlord had many enemies. It was 1609. Japanese armies led by many different warlords were fighting for power. Ikeda needed to be on guard at all times.

Ikeda

Himeji Castle's main tower is about 300 feet tall. That's about half as high as Seattle's Space Needle and St. Louis's Gateway Arch.

Dark figures moved in the shadows below him. These were not attackers. They were his **warriors**, called **samurai** (SAM-oo-*rye*). Three thousand samurai protected Himeji (hee-may-gee) Castle and Ikeda with their lives.

Himeji Castle

A Reward for Ikeda

Almost nine years before, Ikeda had led part of an army that belonged to his wife's father, Tokugawa (toe-koo-gah-wa). The army won an important battle. Tokugawa became the most powerful warlord in Japan. He gave Ikeda Himeji Castle as a reward.

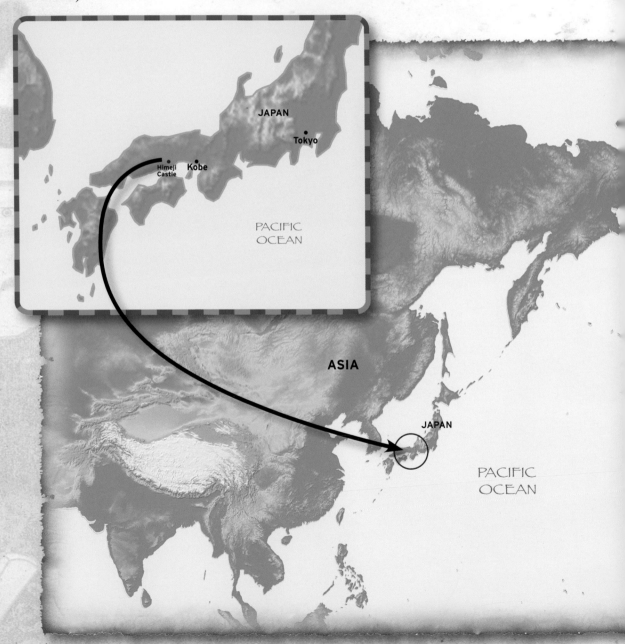

The castle had been standing since the 1300s. First it was a simple fort. Later, different buildings were added and the tower was made higher.

Ikeda knew enemies were near. He decided to make Himeji Castle the strongest castle in Japan. At the same time, he would make it beautiful.

NORTH AMERICA

ATLANTIC OCEAN

In Japanese, Tokugawa was known as **shogun.** He had more power than anyone in Japan besides the **emperor.**

White Crane Castle

Ikeda made the castle bigger and stronger. First, he built a huge stone base for the building. On this base, he built a castle that was wide at the bottom and narrow at the top, like a **pyramid**.

The castle had many levels. Each level had its own roof, which curved and turned up at the end. Ikeda also built a five-story tower. All of the castle's outside walls were plastered white.

At last the tall, graceful building was finished. It looked like a beautiful white bird about to take flight. Himeji Castle became known as White Crane Castle.

During Ikeda's time, castle roofs were covered with stone, clay, lead, or tiles.

The building was so big that Ikeda ran out of wood and stone. He had to use **tombstones** and **coffins** to finish it.

Beautiful and Strong

Himeji Castle was beautiful. Every part of it was made to protect Ikeda. In the sunlight the shining white walls could blind an enemy. The plaster was fireproof and made the walls strong. Arrows would bounce off the curving roofs instead of sticking into them.

The stone base was so tall that an enemy looking up from the bottom couldn't even see the castle. The base blocked the whole sky.

Slits and small openings were cut into the walls. Samurai could throw boiling water and stones through the openings on attackers. They could shoot arrows or bullets through the slits.

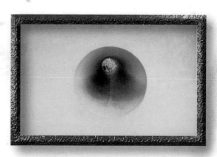

Stones, arrows, and boiling water could be thrown through these holes found in the walls of Himeji Castle.

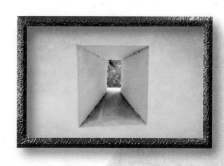

The slits and openings in the castle wall were in many different shapes.

The strong stone base could also hold up the castle in an earthquake. There are many earthquakes in Japan.

11

Grounds for Defense

Attackers might not even get as far as the castle. Ikeda had made it very difficult for enemies to reach it.

Around the castle there were three big ditches filled with water, called **moats**. Enemies would have to unload supplies, carry them across the water, then pack them up again three times before reaching the castle. All this work would tire them out. Supplies would be wet and ruined.

One of 84 gates at Himeji Castle

Beyond the moats were 84 small gates. Only a few men could fit through at once. Samurai hidden behind the gates could shoot those who got through one by one.

A moat at Himeji Castle

Samurai used rifles and bows and arrows to attack their enemies.

Always Ready to Fight

During this time in Japan, samurai were part of the ruling class. Many samurai worked for warlords. They fought well with spears, guns, and bows and arrows. They were also expert fighters with their hands and feet. This kind of fighting is known as **martial** (MAR-shuhl) **arts**.

Samurai in battle

The samurai lived by **harsh** rules. During a battle, they wore heavy **armor**. Even outside a battle, a samurai carried two swords in a sash around his waist. One was long and curving. The other was short. The samurai were ready for anything.

A modern Japanese man dressed in traditional samurai clothing.

If someone didn't bow to a samurai, the samurai could kill him on the spot.

Secrets Inside

Ikeda built the inside of the castle to be ready for anything. Hidden passages connected the main tower with the three smaller towers. If there was an attack, he could escape quickly. The tower had rooms for supplies in case an attack lasted for days.

A hallway in Himeji Castle

The hallways were long and winding. Rows of weapons lined the walls. **Ammunition** was stored at the top of the wall and held up by ropes. It could be pulled down quickly.

Some of the walls had hollow spaces for samurai or **ninjas** to hide inside. There, they would wait to sneak up on **invaders**.

There were always plenty of weapons in case of an attack at Himeji Castle.

From the outside, Himeji Castle is five stories tall. Inside, however, there are six stories. Ikeda may have built it this way to confuse invaders who got inside.

17

Shadow Warriors

Ninjas were not samurai. They were a special part of a warlord's defenses known as "shadow warriors." Ninjas were clever and tricky. Warlords used them to spy and to carry out battle plans.

A ninja performing a secret hand sign

Ikeda's father-in-law, Tokugawa, had used ninjas in different battles. Once, before a big battle, they sneaked into an enemy camp. They added poison to the water. The enemy warriors were too sick to put up a good fight. Tokugawa had no trouble winning.

Many movies have been made about ninjas. This picture is from the movie *Revenge of the Ninja* (1983).

At one time, people thought ninjas could do magic. They thought that ninjas could fly and move things with their minds.

An Amazing Maze

Ikeda died in 1613, four years after completing Himeji Castle. He didn't die in battle. The castle was never attacked.

Ikeda's son became the next lord of the castle, but he died three years later. In 1617, Lord Honda and his family came to live at the castle.

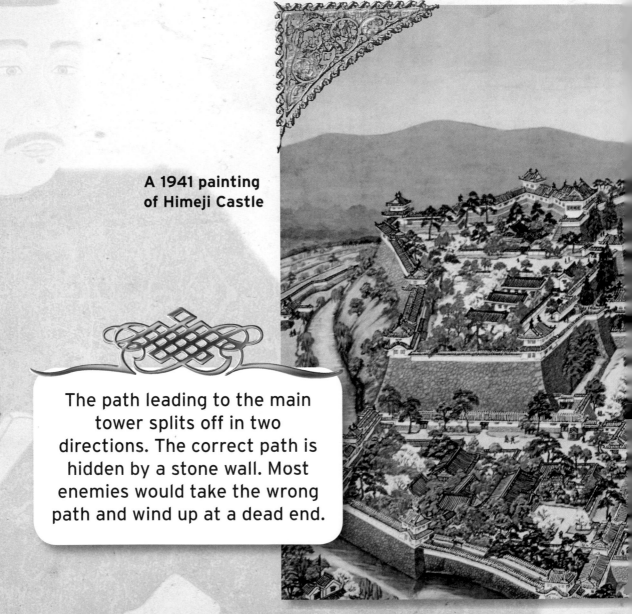

A 1941 painting of Himeji Castle

The path leading to the main tower splits off in two directions. The correct path is hidden by a stone wall. Most enemies would take the wrong path and wind up at a dead end.

Lord Honda made the castle even safer. He built a
maze of pathways on the castle grounds. The pathways
twisted and circled around on three levels. Honda thought
that invaders would become lost on their way to the
castle. While they were stumbling around in the open, the
samurai could attack them.

A Palace for a Princess

Tokugawa's granddaughter, Princess Sen, was married to Lord Honda's son. She and her husband came to live at Himeji Castle, too.

Cosmetic Tower was built for Princess Sen by her father-in-law.

Princess Sen was married at age six or seven. Her husband died in battle 12 years later.

Princess Sen was rich. She brought a lot of money into the Honda family. Lord Honda used some of it to build beautiful new rooms for his son and the princess.

The castle became fancier as the years went on. Rulers added expensive furniture and paintings. It became a palace as well as a **fortress**.

Okiku's Well

Some people think the castle is haunted. A maid named Okiku (oh-kee-koo) heard people planning to kill the lord. She told her samurai boyfriend. He and other samurai stopped the attack.

Okiku's ghost, crying

Okiku's body was found, but the ghostly counting didn't stop until a special temple was built to honor her.

One person who was part of the plan wasn't found out. To get even with Okiku, he stole a dinner plate and blamed it on her. The plate was part of a set of ten. Okiku was punished and killed. Her body was thrown into a well.

People have heard a woman counting from one to ten near the well. They say it's Okiku's ghost, searching for the missing plate.

Visiting Himeji Castle Today

Himeji Castle was never attacked. For that reason, it's the best-kept castle in Japan today.

To visit, take the train to the Himeji station and walk to the castle. Then wander through the maze. You will pass small houses where samurai lived.

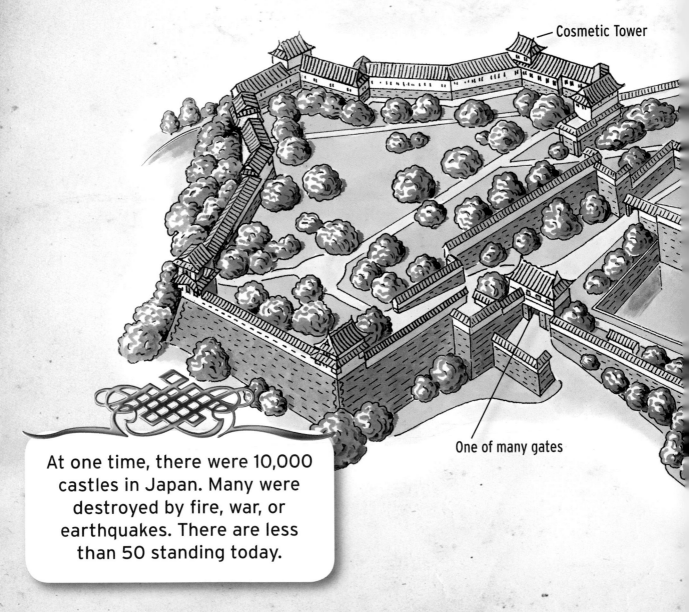

Cosmetic Tower

One of many gates

At one time, there were 10,000 castles in Japan. Many were destroyed by fire, war, or earthquakes. There are less than 50 standing today.

Most of the rooms in the castle are empty. Some show old armor, weapons, and paintings. You can also climb the tower for a beautiful view.

In 1993, Himeji Castle was added to UNESCO's World Heritage List. This group gets money to take care of the castle for Japan and the world to treasure.

Slits and small holes used by the samurai to attack enemies

Main tower

Stone base

Okiku's Well

Moat

Just the Facts

- Before Himeji was built, Japanese castles were usually all made of wood.

- Tokugawa's own castle was in the city of Edo (ay-doe). Later Edo was named Tokyo.

- In Japanese, "jo" means "castle." So Himeji Castle is sometimes called "Himeji-jo."

- A "man day" is how much work a male worker can do in a day. Himeji Castle took about 25 million man days to complete.

- Some people call Himeji "White Heron Castle." Herons are birds that are graceful like the castle.

Timeline

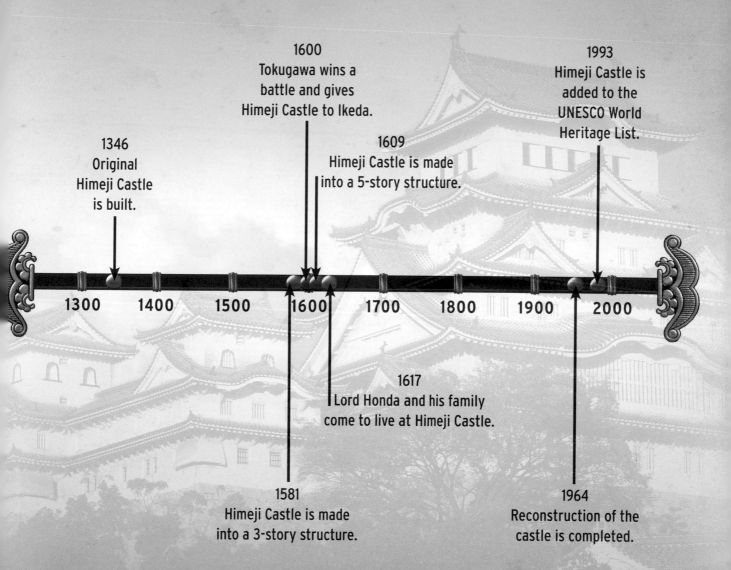

1346
Original
Himeji Castle
is built.

1600
Tokugawa wins a
battle and gives
Himeji Castle to Ikeda.

1609
Himeji Castle is made
into a 5-story structure.

1993
Himeji Castle is
added to the
UNESCO World
Heritage List.

1300 1400 1500 1600 1700 1800 1900 2000

1617
Lord Honda and his family
come to live at Himeji Castle.

1581
Himeji Castle is made
into a 3-story structure.

1964
Reconstruction of the
castle is completed.

Glossary

ammunition (am-yuh-NISH-uhn) the objects fired from weapons, such as bullets or arrows

armor (AR-mur) a suit made of metal worn to protect the body in battle

coffins (KAWF-inz) long boxes in which dead people are buried

emperor (EM-pur-ur) the male ruler of an empire, or group of countries that have the same ruler

fortress (FOR-triss) a large building or area that is strengthened against attacks

harsh (HARSH) cruel or strict

invaders (in-VADE-urz) people who enter a place by force in order to take it over

martial arts (MAR-shuhl ARTS) style of fighting or self-defense

maze (MAYZ) a confusing group of paths that are set up like a puzzle

moats (MOHTS) deep, wide ditches dug around a castle and filled with water for protection against enemies

ninjas (NIN-juhz) people who are experts in ancient Japanese martial arts, especially ones hired as spies

pyramid (PIHR-uh-mid) a stone monument with a square base and triangular sides that meet at a point on top

samurai (SAM-oo-*rye*) a Japanese warrior, or soldier, who lived in medieval times (the years between 500 and 1450)

shogun (SHOH-guhn) supreme military ruler

tombstones (TOOM-*stonez*) blocks of stone that mark graves

warlord (WOR-lord) a military ruler who has power over a certain area

warriors (WOR-ee-urz) soldiers, or people who fight battles

Bibliography

Gravett, Christopher. *Eyewitness Guides: Castle.* New York, NY: Alfred A. Knopf (1994).

Steele, Philip. *Castles.* Boston, MA: Kingfisher (Houghton Mifflin) (1995).

Wilkinson, Philip. *Castles.* New York, NY: Dorling Kindersley (1997).

Read More

Biesty, Stephen. *Stephen Biesty's Castles.* New York, NY: Enchanted Lion Books (2004).

Heinrichs, Ann. *Japan.* New York, NY: Children's Press (1997).

Kimmel, Eric A. *Three Samurai Cats: A Story From Japan.* New York, NY: Holiday House, Inc. (2003).

Learn More Online

Visit these Web sites to learn more about Himeji Castle:

www.columbia.edu/itc/ealac/V3613/himeji/tpage.htm

www.himeji-castle.gr.jp/index/English/

www3.tky.3web.ne.jp/~edjacob/himeji.htm

Index

armor 15, 27
arrows 10–11, 13, 14

battle 6, 14–15, 18–19, 20, 22, 29
building 9

Cosmetic Tower 22, 26

earthquake 11, 26
Edo 28
emperor 7

guns 14

Ikeda 4–5, 6–7, 8–9, 10, 12, 16–17, 19, 20, 29
invaders 17, 21

Japan 6–7, 11, 14, 26–27

Lord Honda 20–21, 22–23, 29

map 6–7
martial arts 14
maze 20–21, 26
moats 12–13, 27

ninjas 17, 18–19

Okiku 24–25, 27

palace 22–23
Princess Sen 22–23

samurai 5, 11, 13, 14–15, 17, 18, 21, 24, 26–27
shogun 7
spears 14
stone base 8, 10–11, 27

Tokugawa 6–7, 19, 22, 28–29
Tokyo 28
tower 4, 7, 8, 16, 20, 27

UNESCO 27, 29

warlord 4, 6, 14, 18
warriors 5, 18–19
White Crane Castle 8–9
White Heron Castle 28

About the Author

Jacqueline A. Ball has written and produced more than
one hundred books for kids and adults.
She lives in New York City and Old Lyme, Connecticut.